Tragic Love: Wrath and Sin

Aracely Reyes

BookLeaf Publishing

Presentation by *BookLeaf Publishing*

Web: www.bookleafpub.com

E-mail: info@bookleafpub.com

ISBN: 978-93-5744-815-4

First edition 2022

DEDICATION

In memory of Jaime Romero, regardless of how chaotic this world has become, I wish you were here to bring the laughter. We need it.

ACKNOWLEDGEMENT

Firstly a big thank you to my dear friend Anjelina, for suggesting that I do this 21 day writing challenge. It was an incredible and deeply rewarding experience. In many ways I feel like myself again. Thank you!
Thank you to BookLeaf Publishing for this amazing opportunity. Thank you to Aluna Theatre, for supporting me as an artist, for being the lightning that re-lit my spark. To my partner Daniel, and my friends: Angela, Jennifer, Raquel, Zee, Belinda, Tiffy, Shohra, and Steven, thank you for accepting me, believing in me, cheering me on for so many years now. I am the luckiest goth girl in the world. Your love means everything to me. To Neals and the Hernandez family, thank you for treating me as if I was your own. You owed me nothing, and gave me everything, a family. I love you all.
To my co-workers, Tammy and Laura; Be warned, here comes another piece that will make you cry. I'm sorry. My intentions are to tell my stories, after years of being forced to hold everything back. I can't, not anymore, or ever again.
Lastly, to you my readers, thank you for giving me another chance, to continue to walk with me

on this twisted journey. We are all unfinished.
We are all seeking the same things: acceptance
and love, from everyone, and mostly from
ourselves.

PREFACE

After Tragic Love, the plan was always to publish another book. Not only was there plenty of material left over, but through the challenges and eye opening realities of publishing, I remain very proud of a novel that I created when I was at my absolute lowest. I have come a long way from the frustrated, heart broken, drained, and often hopeless student-artist. Adulthood hit me hard. Right in the back of my head, and launched me into roaring flames. I now see myself as a charred, black phoenix-swan, perhaps visibly damaged, strange to the world, but I have grown to accept this strange, scared form. I accept me.

Then, the pandemic hit. I was about to re-enter the world of art. Not that I ever really left, but it wasn't paying my bills. I took on an ordinary trade to move, to pay my student loans, and so on. In 2020, I became an "essential worker" with no other choice but to stand in the front lines. I went from applying to Circus school, to suiting up to face disease, fear, and exhaustion, at everything. Many lives, including mine, were put on hold. Almost two years later and very little has changed sadly.

When a dear friend of mine suggested this 21 day writing challenge, I jumped at the chance to create and publish again. I didn't know how much I needed this until I was on day ten. It would have been so easy to take the pieces I already had left over, waiting to be presented to the world, but after everything I've seen, heard, and experienced during two of the most chaotic years of my existence; I had to write everything. The tragedy of seeking, maintaining, treasuring, and nurturing love continues, even in the midst of a crumbling world. At the same time, I acknowledge and am grateful to say that the losses I suffered were mental, psychological, and emotional, but thankfully nothing physical. My loved ones have survived, and so have I. I cry for the many others who haven't been as lucky. I can't imagine not just the heartbreak, but also the raw, ongoing pain of losing someone to a seemingly unstoppable force, and trying to continue on in the midst of misunderstanding and hate. There is such a lack of compassion, and unfortunately I don't have anywhere near enough to make an impact. But, I want to try. My struggle now is how to continue to be grateful for what I have, the people I can, if not now, hopefully in the immediate future speak to, see face to face, and embrace. But, at the same time I am angry, I am frustrated, I am tired, and I am deeply afraid.

This is my exploration of what I went through these past two years. Brace yourself. At least you get a warning.

~Welcome back to the Abyss

Fellow sadists and masochists, your attention is appreciated.
Step through the curtain, and feast your eyes.
Behold the tale of a split, choking world.
Just a few months into the New Year,
Murderous plagues rampaged, death tolls surged.
Middle-aged, bleached, banshee zombies rose.
Fires and storms hammered the planet,
And tyranny took over the thrones.
Existence seemed futile, and resistance a lifestyle.
Faith in humanity diminishes, as resources are purged.
Petty battles declared, in public, in private, in vain.
The narcissistic abandoning the world for the web,
Every individual, suddenly boxed in, on their own.
It is during these times, where roles are flipped.
Artists walk through the mirror,

And become miserable labourers.
The dreamers turn into pessimists.
Hope fades, the angrier humans become.
The greedy become more desperate,
Masquerading as "Police officers," "Tax
investigators,"
Your "long lost grandson," your "hot, young
boyfriend."
Roles are changing, but for the worse.
The world is in a sorry state, for the vulnerable,
Not more so, but premonitions come true.
A world abused, robbed, raped, and pillaged
must die.
This is always how the tale, the performance
would end.
Therefore, the world, as a whole must change.
But we are sculpting its evolution.
The final product always carries the artist's
signature.
It may already be too late, all signs point to the
end.
A painful end, where we will leave this plane
starving.
Burnt from a desert in our stomachs and veins.
Our bodies gasping, convulsing, impaled with
tubing.
Crying out for relatives, and friends long gone.

~Distorted

Human flesh is imperfect.
It is soft, fragile, supple, easily marred and
mangled.
Distorted, most of all.
How it twists. Oh, how it stings. How it cracks.
And I, more so. I am a strange creature.
So much, it is so easy to simply see me as just.
Easy to forget that I am also human,
A mangled, putrid green abomination.
Always in the way. Always so obvious.
Always so eager to remind you of everything
you hate.
Everything you fear. Everything you want to
deny.
And before I would curl up, wordless.
Motionless.
But no more.
I will be obscene, and force my fractured way
into your view.
You will see my brokenness. My distort.
You may gag. You may fuck off.
But you will never forget the sight of the
monster that is me.
Forever burnt in your mind, mortality.
Weakness, but I shall ascend strong.

I curse you. My revenge now so.
Perhaps only I can see myself, my form as
beautiful.
My twisted, shattered, fractured, coiled,
Bended, shot in, strangled, splintered,
Distorted. I am human, distorted.
And so are you.

~Set me on fire

My nightmares retell of my assault,
It happened indoors, during an autumn month.
The nightmares are darkness, but I hear the
screaming.
It is preferred; otherwise an orange blade would
flash,
Just missing my face, the arm being pulled back.
The demon wailing, forcibly dragged back.
Yes, the shock and trembles of horror plague my
body,
But a stronger, forbidden emotion sweeps over.
A cold, heavy lava is poured over my head,
By the time it reaches my feet I am incensed.
I want blood, I want broken limbs, I want
slaughter.
This attack grew from infant teasing, to
chauvinistic taunting.
A familiar tale of being a woman under
employment,
My reports were handled as exaggerations
unimportant.
The insults continued, and then came the
staking.
Finally, a threat was made, and the uppercuts
took action.

It unleashed the monster, free and eager to exact
revenge.
Yet, in the moment, I had to remain frozen.
The beast was allowed to antagonize the lesser
sex,
But if I had fought back, put up my arms,
pushed back,
I would have been unwaged. I would have been
chained.
Recovery was near impossible, returning to the
crime scene daily.
I am asked to forget, begged to forgive and serge
forward.
Continue to work through the injustice, play
invisible.
I regret not retaliating; at least there'd be some
satisfaction.
There was no anguish in his eyes, only entitled
hate.
I want pain, I want suffering, I want retribution.
I'd castrate, and gift him a vagina if I could.
I'd cut him from side to side, and shove a fist in.
I live day by day, with anger and frustration.
But I live, as I am reminded to be so grateful.
I am living, I am employed, and life must carry
on.
I dull the audio flashbacks with small yellow
pills,

But nothing to numb the trembles, or strengthen
my core.
Therefore, with gritted teeth, I march into the
office,
My anger always at the surface, with a single
goal.
I will continue to survive, amongst all the liars,
Who gladly would've have allowed me,
A hysterical, insane, frail woman to fuckin' die.

~Show me Victim blaming

"They're just having a bad day."
A day so bad, they went out of their way
To tell me, to eat my own entrails and die?
A day so bad, their fists met my head,
In hard, hot pounds that buckled my feet.
A day so bad, I was reminded I'm just
A mindless slave, a capitalist whore,
A flea diseased ox, on the end of a spiked whip.
I am nothing, feel nothing, and do as I'm told.
"So, hurry up and get that before I smash your
face in!"
It must be a bad day.
A day so bad, the only way to feel any pleasure,
Was to attack a pitiful, exploited employee.
To remind them how degrading it is to stand up
to you,
And still assist in your purchases, even carry
your items.
It's my fault. I chose to be poor, chose to get that
loan,
So now my profession involves daily assaults.
But I don't call them that, never in public.
After all: "The customer is always right".

~My body snatcher

I'm glaring at my permanent, protruding ribs,
Disgusted that they're there, and it's still not
enough.
I'm shaking, knowing I have to eat a spoonful,
Just a spoonful, and the two hundred pound
monster
Will burst out of my stomach, eat my thin frame,
Bones, hair, tattoos, claws, intestines, and all.
And she'll replace me. She'll be my true form.
The trembles are worse, shedding insane driven
tears.
I don't want to eat, and fulfill everyone's
premonition.
"You're going to get fat." "Your clothes are
going to shrink."
"Watch what you eat, watch how much you eat."
"Did you get your steps in today? Are you
summer bod ready?"
"It just happens, you get fat, and then you'd be
better off dead."
The hot tears sting, as my stomach begins to stab
me.
The years of purging have already taken hold,

If I don't feed the beast, it will, must feed on
me!
Joylessly, in the fashion of a ravenous zombie,
I scarf down my meal, and I resent myself for
every bite.
I curl up tightly once I've licked my plate clean
like a pig.
I think of myself as a gross, fat maggot, always
hungry,
Always worthless, always bound to mindlessly
to eat.
When I was a child, I saw myself as the fat
worm,
And dreamt of one day peeling my nasty flesh,
And turning into a beautiful, strong, brave
butterfly.
But I know now that it's never going to happen.
I'm bound to this body, chained to my mind that
hates it.

~Let me take a selfish moment: Bye Toxicia

Let me indulge at being just an asshole,
Because frankly that's all you've been to me,
And I've never had the pleasure, or a shot.
Sorry, (Not sorry), but I have to be blunt,
I never liked you, and I pretended a lot!
I saw you, like what, every six months?
So now, honestly, I don't give a fuck.
Sue me for being an absolute bitch,
But we both know we were never friends, sis.
I felt you were blah, and you hated my guts,
And my hair, and my games, and my books,
Written by all those "talentless fem-authors".
And my favourite movies, and my clothes,
And my boyfriend, (Yep, he knows.)
But, can you be honest, and say you hate me?
Take the time as I am now, just admit it.
I promise it's so liberating, even cathartic!
Always eager to inject everything I loved,
With your brand of appropriated "arsenico".

You always hated me, that's why I never met the
fiancé.
No wedding invite for Cely, whoopsie, my bad!
You didn't have the patience, bitch, I never had
patience!
I was nice to you. I'm never nice to anyone!
Except my friends, you know, folks who don't
judge moi.
Don't roll their eyes, snap their know-it-all
heads .
Yes, I'm calling you out, 'cause if we were
friends,
You were a piss poor, a piss poor friend.
I was pleasant with you, even at the end.
I wished you well, open to being civil.
The cowardly, dead silence is sooo you,
And yeah, the musing is proof
You got to me, under my skin, not cool.
'Cause no matter what : I look like shit.
I thought we were friends, yeah weird.
I didn't know the jokes gone too far,
Was you repeatedly, telling me to piss off.
It was always going to be my damn fault,
Because you're passive aggressive
And I am never passive "sister".
So now, I'm going to just be petty,
Because, you were always a bastard.
And I sat there, in shame, in silence, waiting.
Waiting for you to calm the hell down,

Waiting for you to just STFU woman!
My Gods! I could've clocked you for being
negative,
All the gosh darn damn time!
Could've clocked you for never having the time
to unwind,
But managed to snag and keep a man, hot dang!
Couldn't be bothered to nurture your
friendships,
"Can't stand humanity" your "introvertness" .
Well yes, I am very much like humanity
And I have feelings, and we share friends,
Who I love more than anything
On this cold, cruel, dark, awful planet.
I never liked you, but I fucking tried!
And the one thing I wish, if you had just said so,
Instead, behind insults, shaming, and lies,
You tortured me,
Every chance you got.
EVERY CHANCE YOU GOT.

~Mask and unmask

Gagged and restrained, a barrier, like a muzzle.
But I embraced the mandatory disguise.
The caution tape over our mouths and noses;
"Stay back, stay away. I could make you sick."
Suddenly perverts were no longer interested.
Getting lucky wasn't worth contracting plague.
Overnight the world was coming to an end,
And it was finally safe to be out alone.
Better than mace, more threatening than a
switchblade
A piece of cloth, covering half of my face.
"Stay back, stay away. I cough, you may die."
Had I known years ago, something so simple.
I'd ride the subway every night, sip my latte in
peace.
No one dares to sit beside, across, or behind.
No expectations to smile, say hi, act "nice".
"Stay back, stay away. Stay back, stay away."
Sad really, what it took, to leave all strangers
alone.
It may be selfish, to see the silver lining at this
time,
But isn't the saying: "Count your blessings?"
Being masked has never made me feel safer,
From disease, and from monstrous beasts.

~eyE droP

I don't care if the scars on the wrists stain.
I'll slice your wire again and again.
I will not make you laugh. I cannot bring you
joy.
I will be the clown that glares at you in the toy
box;
A damning reminder that innocence is a lie.
I will make you scream. I will make you cry.
I will remind you every day and night,
That we only live to grow old and die.
And all the way through, the colours of joys,
Mix, distort, and mush into putrid grey.
The taste of candy fades away to cavities,
The simmering balloons pop to soil toxins.
Dreams are unattainable, like that of a happy
clown.
We are monsters. Anti-humans, painted demons.
All your shame is embodied in us. All your
failures.
All your faults and deformities, masqueraded for
your pleasure.
For your mockery; all hail the clown never.
We exist so you can be proud,
For no one is lower, or lesser than the clown.

Prepare yourself then, for my tale of revenge.
Like the jesters, my predecessors, who were said
to go mad,
Breaking their smeared smiles and slaughtering
their masters.
But they were not insane; they simply fought
back.
And showed humans the real monsters, the great
puppet masters.
I am that clown, the clown that will drive you
mad.
The clown that will be made a fool of never
more.
The clown, who will be said to have gone mad,
But only after I have showed you all that I am.

~ Hail October

It sounds cliché: the goth Latina, witch-bruja
adores,
The mid-autumn month, when day becomes
more night.
When the trees bleed orange-red leaves that
gather beneath.
When it's acceptable to embrace grotesque decor
and clothing,
In exchange for gluttony, greed, and children's
play shrieks.
I have my morbid celebrations: Dia de los
muertos and séances.
The celebration of the dying sun; Samhain, all
Hallows Eve.
I also have the more mundane pleasures, like
pumpkin spice tea,
Sweet harvest pies, warm maple syrup, crunchy
tart apples.
The truth is I thrive in the hot summer months
with sunshine.
Unburden by heavy clothing, suffocating scarves
and boots.
Savoring sweet, cool drinks and planting
precious seeds.

I mourn the end of the simple months with the understanding,
That the decay arriving is necessary, and part of the cycle.
Life and death waltz in autumn, death taking the lead.
The time when the world stands still, frozen death, at rest,
Comes after the colourful blood bath, when the sun falls.
I despise the Winter, but I've come to love the brief change before,
Where everyone is a Latte-aficionado, orange is trendy,
Everyone is a demon, wolf, goblin, or witch like me.
Where I don't have to justify being spooky, I just belong.
 A final hurrah, before the lonely, long cold months arrive.
Hail autumn, hail candy, hail death and memory,
Hail October! Hail October! Hail October! All Hail!

~ Walking through an abandoned graveyard

Eventually, even the dearly departed,
Beneath tall, polished stones will be forgotten.
That is an unquestionable truth, during a trip,
Through an abandoned, lonely graveyard.
The pathway through the chipped sepulchres,
Is cracked, uneven, and the spaces filled with grass.
Large, grey and white mushrooms have taken over,
Their edges are covered in dripping black pus.
The tears of the lost and putrefied souls remaining,
Residing under fallen over, and vandalized tombs.
The land is decrypted, only fruitful to fungi and filth.
The newest corpse buried here is from 1864th.
Imagine the thousands spent on the plots,
The engraved names and dates on the smooth rock.

All for naught, as pieces of the memorials,
Lie under the mangled trees and bushes.
Any visitors by-pass the crumbling park,
And travel through the nearby shopping mall,
Or arrive and enter their apartments and houses.
Neglected, only the morbidly addicted or the
desperate,
Acknowledge this portal to the land of the dead
and fallen.
The abandoned cadavers have only to look
forward,
To being paved over, transformed into a store or
home,
To participate in current, selfish, oblivious life.
The new, constant visitors, unknowingly
trampling,
The dead, the damned, the redeemed, and the
saved.

~ "Choosing Violence"

One does not simply choose violence,
At least that is not the case for me.
To be honest, sometimes it is a reflex,
In a moment of stress, in the face of aggression.
Pent up anger from getting teased as a kid,
Being bullied at home from the "perfect"
sibling.
Forced shame at being difficult, headed for Hell.
I was taught to shut up and not fight back.
Don't make it worse, be friends, be nice.
I don't know how most adults turn out,
From years of being subjected to harassment,
And being repeatedly forced to just accept it.
I can only state that it unlocked wrath in me.
I would not just take it, I would not be quiet!
Truth be told, I wasn't built for a passive society.
I belong in the days when problems were solved,
By wielding an axe, and swinging it into heads.
Obviously I recognize that doesn't solve
problems,
But I think people would think before speaking,
If they knew the consequences would be painful.

It's interesting that in the age of "going viral",
Me choosing to tell a harasser to back the hell
off,
Is tagged as "that insane lady chose violence."
It is a testament of how submissive when
convenient
This world I am trying to survive in has become.
Let's not forget, certain folks can "choose
violence",
And when it's someone like me, who is never
allowed
To even speak up, say stop, say no, fight back,
It's seen as violence, as an unspeakable, harmful
act.

~Worry time

The strangest venture I have taken upon,
Is setting time to sit and ponder troubles.
I am asked to list my concerns and fears,
The troubles I encountered during the day,
The dangers I may face the very next day.
I recall my anxieties over failure and shame.
I remember how I have to carry a blade,
For walks at dawn and dusk, to get to work,
And for the lonely travels back to my home.
I think about the people I've encountered,
The ones who aren't friends or even cordial.
I sob over the people I must at all costs avoid,
Strangers, enemies, backstabbing colleagues.
People who I know will only bring me harm,
Who I may I fail to stay away from, but I'll try.
I worry about sudden death, I fret over illnesses.
I obsess over accidents, acts of God unforeseen
I cry over all the things I cannot control.
I end up in a helpless lump, cold, dreadful,
alone.
I remain as such for several minutes, my tears,
They flow out of my body like poisoned blood,
Slipping, dripping, buckets and pools of it.
And once I am drained, I finally stand and walk.
Now that all my concerns have been bled out,

What's left is simply hope. A wish for the better.
A desire that I do have some control of my
journey.
That I can be strong enough to all that upsets
me.
I may not leave the battles unscarred, but I'll
leave.
I am grateful that I survived, and ask that I may
continue.
Even if I must perform this horrific ritual over
again,
I want to live tomorrow, to worry, to wonder, to
hope.

~ Muñeca

(Muñeca is part of the Theatrical play Muñeca,
and a short film, featured in the CAMINOs 2021
Theatre festival.)
Mother named me Muñeca, shortly after birth.
The name stayed throughout my childhood,
And in and out I was played with and cherished,
Until a newer model took away my place.
I remember a time I resented the name,
Everyone else was "precious" or "treasure",
And I was named after a plaything,
That would grow old, worn, and one day;
Be forgotten or thrown away.
Luckily, when I saw myself deteriorate,
I gathered my rags and ran away.
I wasn't a cute little doll anymore,
I was a rebellious young woman,
That my mother grew to hate.
Like all things, the name sounds better
In Spanish, rather than plain English;
Muñeca, Muñeca, Soy Muñeca.
Ever since I was forgotten and replaced,
I have surrounded myself with dozens,
On dozens of mini mes, big and small.
They fill my shelves high on my walls,
But none of their sweet faces,

Can fill the catacombs in my heart.

26

~Wraith is my sin

Of all the deadly sins,
The least I understand,
Is the one tied to emotion,
Not an act, an intention.
One can stop themselves,
From stealing, cheating.
You can hold your tongue,
Before swearing; Oh my God.
But anger simply happens,
It is a reaction, unbridled.
It was turned into a sin,
As a means to control.
Like women, reproduction,
Thoughts and feelings,
Threaten God's plan.
Anger acknowledges harm,
It helps one process pain,
And not become a victim,
And never, ever give up.
I don't care if my sin is rage,
I wield it like a shield and blade.
Religion won't scare me,
I will not be abused,
I will not be dragged to Hell.

~Prodigy

As a child, I was pushed, pulled constantly.
As an adult, I am deemed:
An utter waste as woman/offspring.
"I will not have a stupid child."
" A talentless child."
" A blasphemy. "
"You must be an artist!"
"It's time to practice."
"Do as I, exactly, perfectly."
"Pray. No, not like that!"
"Do it again."
Adolescence, I never pleased my makers.
Who birthed me "by accident",
Because God told them they had to.
Frustrations, to earn their pride.
But I accept, if I am to create,
I must, and earn my self worth.
I settled on what I enjoyed
And would gain much skill,
Throughout, the beings
I owed my existence to:
We are never happy,
Never satisfied,
Never proud,
Maybe never loved.

It explains my morbid fascinations,
The need to capture it constant.
Nonetheless, I have found pleasure
In my desperate musings,
Found satisfaction in my blood,
And sweat soaked canvas.
If I submitted to the failed aspirations,
I would have given up,
And crawled into a cubicle to die.
I remain determined,
Slightly boastful,
And eccentric.
My coffin tributes,
The ghost in my pages
applauds my efforts,
As do I.

~The Pandemic: Essential Worker

The world was forced to shutter,
Except labourers as I; worker essential.
Instead of isolation, I faced throngs.
Horrifying trips on crowded buses,
Face to face with the screaming maskless.
The world was suffering, none by choice.
My choices were to work and maybe die,
And yes I'd prefer to stay home, alone,
Lock down from others, and stay alive.
Not sure it's worth human interactions,
To pay bills, wiping spit from my shield.
Frustrating to justify, earning from home,
Surely I must risk my flesh and sanity.
Yes, I was deemed a hero in politics,
'Til the demands for more wages brewed.
It's no wonder so many of my brethren,
Gave up, pulled back, deserted the frontlines,
Forever known as the cowardly lazy,
The instigators of the "labour shortage".
Neither those who left, or those who stay,
Do so out of selfishness or simple greed.

We are exhausted, and deeply afraid,
We are working for survival,
And could die regardless.
We are feeding the ravenous,
Healing the angry and the stubborn.
Calming those enraged and ignorant,
A thankless job, turned loathed by all.
Whatever end of the pandemic,
The fate of work essential will change.
Folks as I will not emerge silent.
Give us our dignity, or choke, literally.

~I weep for my guardian angel

I weep for my guardian angel,
For I have cursed his meat and spirit.
For an angel who loves a wicked mortal,
Filled with yearnings, to take pleasure from
revenge,
His love for me, a wrench human.
Has tainted his wings, broken with ink.
Damned forever, till all his white feathers fall
away.
I can offer only trials, tests because I doubt,
That you want me. That I am worth your soul.
I have always admired you for being selfless,
For striving to care for me, heal my wounds.
Right my wrongs, pray my antlers turn halo.
My anger gives me away however,
My envy at the ease of everyone around me.
Success never coming easy, joyless as always.
You my angel, are my only guiding light,
My fear is I am your only purpose,
And I am molding you to only become mine.
Do I complete you? Can you rescue me?
I am afraid that I cannot grow with you,

And learn why you love me, only that I feel the
same.
Is that selfish, or simply just enough?
Can you be satisfied abandoning heaven,
To spend all eternity, in the land of the sick,
The sinful, the dying, to wake with me always?

~Zombie Heart

Denial: Waking to a near empty cavern in my chest.
Rolling over to forget the sleepless night in tears.
Not heartless, not hurting, not angst, better off alone.
Guilt: I cut out what remained, the pain was obvious.
What came was shame, weakness, my wish to return.
To undo the mutilations, further attempts to erase.
Anger: I sought to avenge my dead heart, growing thorns,
Snarling, clawing at strangers, foes, family, even friends.
The world created its demon, I would destroy both.
Bargaining: I went to sleep praying I wouldn't wake.
I begged the light not to coax my eyes, revive the memories.
I'll stop spreading loathing, don't re-grow my heart.

Depression: Nothing was relieving the cold, the
ringing.
What remained was dead, dry, the roots of a
burnt forest.
There was no moving on, simply watching the
decay.
Reconstruction: Famously the heart was
exhumed.
The undead resurrection oozed, writhed in my
hip.
With it came understanding, this was forever.
Acceptance: That my hallowed heart remains.
It cannot regenerate, the scars are memories,
The gashes are lessons stabbed in and learned.

~When Happy stories end

I don't quite remember when I stopped smiling
in public,
I know I was still a child when every reply was
with a scowl.
My joy was beaten out of me, trust bullied into
suppression.
Divorced religion. When told God hated me,
heaven closed.
I can't ignore how sorrowful it becomes, when
all thoughts,
All poems, all plays, all books, all drawings, all
paintings,
Reflections of the non-fictional, reflect
loneliness and pain.
I do so perhaps out of cowardness, but also of
pessimism,
A monster has been created, its antagonists
deserve no mercy.
But a monster who remains so by choice, has
only two options,
To hide away from everyone, or eat anyone who
draws near.

As years roll on by, my choice to suppress in
rage is justified,
People are more interested in ridiculing than
being kind.
In being right, than being compassionate, or
helpful.
I no longer care if I am seen as the monster, only
that I live,
That I survive long past these villains, and see
the sun set.

~I am a sinner

A sinner, a wicked being,
A monster, a demon,
A witch, a banshee,
That's how I'm seen.
But I know myself,
And I know I may be
A sinner, a flawed being,
However, I spell it
H.U.M.A.N.
A woman, a fem-being,
A warrior, a survivor,
A dreamer, an artist,
A spiritualist, a medium.
How I see me,
How I know myself to be.
I have made mistakes,
Some beyond repair,
Some beyond reason,
Even forgiveness.
I am not perfect,
Not pretty, not special,
But I am me, and I am
Not a monster, or a demon.
I am a witch, but not evil.
I will make mistakes,

But I am learning, healing.
I am capable of loving,
I am capable of getting better.
I am a sinner, a sinner worth
Standing tall, standing redeemed.

~Pressing on

The options are to die or survive,
My aching flesh urges me forward:
Do not give up, to pain, to fear.
Do not cower, submit to dread.
None know what lies beyond,
This lonely, vast, dying planet.
But until I draw my final breath,
I cherish every minute, hour,
Day, week, month and year alive,
See the world awaken from
The slumber and dark of winter.
To witness the new humans,
In sweet, chubby, round forms,
With nothing but innocence,
In their eyes, their coos, their grins.
To witness a stranger, step forward,
Protect another, or pay for their meal.
I may have cut myself off from evil,
I may have lost hope, but it can renew.
In the time it takes to stay alive,
I can also use the time to watch,
To wait for fellow humans to touch,
To feel the warm sun and remember;
Our purpose is to care and take care,
Of the planet, and each other,

Of the present, of tomorrow.
In spite of the trials and horrors,
I have seen miracles and love,
And I wish to see more. More.

www.ingramcontent.com/pod-product-compliance
Lightning Source LLC
LaVergne TN
LVHW021259200726
843509LV00012B/1720